UNCLONED LIFE

Seven Epic (**Un**)Rules for Owning Your Shit

AUDRIA RICHMOND

Copyright

UnCloned Life

Seven Epic (UnRules) for Owning Your Shit

By

Audria Richmond

Founder and CEO of Building BIG Brands Agency

and UnCloned Life

COPYRIGHT ©2017 BUILDING BIG BRANDS PUBLISHING

ALL RIGHTS RESERVED

All rights reserved. No part of this publication may be reproduced, distributed, or transmitted in any form or by any means, including photocopying, recording, or other electronic or mechanical methods, without the prior written permission of the publisher, except in the case of brief quotations embodied in critical reviews and certain other noncommercial uses permitted by copyright law. For permission requests, email the publisher, addressed "Attention: Permissions Coordinator," at the email below.

Building BIG Brands Publishing

info@buildingbigbrands.com

www.audriarichmond.com

www.uncloned.life

Ordering Information:

Special discounts are available on quantity purchases by corporations, associations, and others. For details, contact the publisher at the email address above.

Orders by U.S. trade bookstores and wholesalers. Please contact Building BIG Brands Publishing:

Tel: (901) 238-6859; or visit **www.audriarichmond.com**

(Paperback)

ISBN 13: 978-0-9980722-2-7

ISBN 10: 0-9980722-2-2

Developmental Editing by: Stefanie Manns

Book Cover Design by: Rochelle Washington

Interior Book Design by: Audria Richmond

Photography by: Christopher Jamar Payne

Fashion Styling by: Rochelle Washington

Table of Contents

Acknowledgments

Join The UnCloned Life Tribe

Introduction

(Un)Rule One
Recall Everything They've Ever Told You
(And Then Forget It)

(Un)Rule Two
Embrace Change

(Un)Rule Three
Always Trust The Person Who Knows
You Best. Yourself.

(Un)Rule Four
Become Your Alter Ego

(Un)Rule Five
To Hell With The Invites From The Cool Kids.
You Weren't Going Anyway.

(Un)Rule Six
Question The Questions

(Un)Rule Seven
Unniche Your Life

Acknowledgments

We are going to make history and change lives with this book! I can feel it and believe it with all of my soul. I want to say thank you to all of my tribe which includes family, friends, clients, customers, and community of people who have watched my business thrive over the past nine years.

This movement all started when Kim Weathersby came onto my Periscope and said **"No Clone Zone"** in the chat comments. You don't even understand the magic that happened from that day forward. **#Uncloned** started as a hashtag and now it's a movement, lifestyle, and brand. This is just the beginning, and you are a part of it because you are reading this book right now.

I want to say a special thanks to Stefanie Manns. This book would not even be possible if she did not work her magic. She has done an amazing job at articulating my voice and helping me craft my message. If you are ever in need of a TRUE PROFESSIONAL, be sure to visit her on the web at www.wordsbystef.com.

Thanks so much again for agreeing to join the movement, and I can't wait to help you UnClone Your LIFE!

#UnClonedLife

Join the Tribe

We have a **FREE** Online Tribe created just for your UnCloned Life. Come and share your thoughts, ideas, and viewpoints with us in the group and social media. You will find access to UnCloned Life content, events, experts, activities, courses, and much more.

JOIN NOW AT

WWW.UNCLONEDTRIBE.LIFE

I paused who I was, to help you become who you were never going to be.

-Janae' Griggs

Introduction

#UNCLONED THOUGHTS

PLEASE DOCUMENT YOUR UNCLONED THOUGHTS HERE.
THIS IS YOUR SAFE SPACE

_____

_____

_____

_____

_____

_____

_____

_____

_____

_____

_____

_____

_____

INTRODUCTION

Once upon a time there was a sorta-sweet little girl named Audria.

With big, poufy hair and a big, bright smile, she grew up with dreams of running the world. An artist to her core, she saw the world in bright, bold colors. Letting her imagination run wild, she would draw anything on everything. She wrote, she danced, and she played freely. She thought she could be whoever and whatever she wanted to be. *Beautiful. Smart. Brave.* She believed she could be anything. Until someone told her she couldn't.

So she stopped being like her and started being like them. She stopped leading and started following. She stopped conjuring and started conforming. She stopped trusting herself and started second guessing. *Everything.*

For years and years, she pretended to be someone else.

#UNCLONED THOUGHTS

PLEASE DOCUMENT YOUR UNCLONED THOUGHTS HERE.
THIS IS YOUR SAFE SPACE

INTRODUCTION

She grew up and, instead of growing into her own woman, she became a replica of the people around her. She spoke like they spoke and moved like they moved. She became conscious and aware of what others thought, often to the detriment of the woman who she so desperately wanted to be. She went with the flow, but somewhere, deep inside, she knew that this life that she lived, this way that she'd been programmed, wasn't true to who she was created to be. She knew there was no way in hell she was made for *this*—to be a captive of the world's way of doing anything. She knew she could no longer ignore the screaming voice in her head that urged her to set it all free, to move with reckless abandon and without inhibition.

Then one day, she realized exactly what she needed to do.

She reared her head back to look up at the starry, night sky.

#UNCLONED THOUGHTS

PLEASE DOCUMENT YOUR UNCLONED THOUGHTS HERE.
THIS IS YOUR SAFE SPACE

_____

_____

_____

_____

_____

_____

_____

_____

_____

_____

_____

_____

INTRODUCTION

Raising a clenched fist in the air, she bellowed the three words that would release her spirit and ignite her soul forevermore.

"FUCK. THE. WORLD!"

And, just like that, she was herself—again. She became a heroine. She became a woman with her own mind, her own thoughts, her own breath, her own roar. She became a ball of fearless fire.

She became UnCloned.

#UNCLONED THOUGHTS

PLEASE DOCUMENT YOUR UNCLONED THOUGHTS HERE.
THIS IS YOUR SAFE SPACE

_____

_____

_____

_____

_____

_____

_____

_____

_____

_____

_____

_____

_____

_____

_____

INTRODUCTION

"You take the **blue pill**, the story ends. You wake up in your bed and believe whatever you want to believe. You take the **red pill**, you stay in Wonderland, and I show you how deep the rabbit hole goes."

-- **Morpheus**

#UNCLONED THOUGHTS

PLEASE DOCUMENT YOUR UNCLONED THOUGHTS HERE.
THIS IS YOUR SAFE SPACE

_____

_____

_____

_____

_____

_____

_____

_____

_____

_____

_____

_____

_____

_____

INTRODUCTION

I used to be just like you.

Unsure. Unconfident. UnMe.

I know it may be hard to believe, but I wasn't always this bodacious being that bursts onto your social media feed with her big brain and bigger ideas. While the thoughts were always there, the boldness wasn't. There was a time in my life when I was thoroughly confused about who I was and how I needed to show up in the world. I was always teetering on the edge of doubt, wandering around in the woods of the wills.

Will the really cool girls like me?

Will these people get it?

Will they actually buy this?

#UNCLONED THOUGHTS

PLEASE DOCUMENT YOUR UNCLONED THOUGHTS HERE.
THIS IS YOUR SAFE SPACE

_____

_____

_____

_____

_____

_____

_____

_____

_____

_____

_____

_____

_____

_____

INTRODUCTION

Whenever I would shake off the fear and silence the questions in one area of my life, it would show up in another. In my work, in my marriage, and in my health. The bottom line was I didn't trust my own value or my own voice. I hid from anything that felt like the spotlight, despite the fact that I'd more than earned my right to be there. Consumed with other people's opinions, thoughts, and ideas, I was nothing that I needed to be and everything everyone else expected me to be. It wasn't as if anyone physically stood over me and beat me over the head until I submitted to their will, but my subconscious was invaded and bombarded with messages of conformity. My reasoning, my religion, and my reflection weren't my own. Those pieces of me were a result of what I thought I should do and what my parents, family, and society thought I should be.

#UNCLONED THOUGHTS

PLEASE DOCUMENT YOUR UNCLONED THOUGHTS HERE.
THIS IS YOUR SAFE SPACE

INTRODUCTION

I was insecure and uncertain about myself—a prisoner to perception.

Eventually, it clicked for me that there was no way I could really be happy and live a never-ordinary life

until I set myself completely free. I had to embrace the truth that I'd always known—that I was not like everybody or anybody else. I was destined to be one-of-a-kind, *Unattached* and *Unhinged*. I was destined to show the world the power that comes with being out of synch with society and fighting, with every fiber of your being, for what you believe in. I was destined to be free.

So freedom became the oxygen I needed to breathe. Being like everybody else became my point of no return. Once I started walking away from that place, I would never look back. The final destination on that passage is the book you

#UNCLONED THOUGHTS

PLEASE DOCUMENT YOUR UNCLONED THOUGHTS HERE.
THIS IS YOUR SAFE SPACE

_____

_____

_____

_____

_____

_____

_____

_____

_____

_____

_____

_____

_____

INTRODUCTION

are holding in your hands.

I believe there is a part of you that has been waiting for this moment. It's that moment when you finally loose yourself from all of the weight that comes with trying to fit in. It's that moment when you reject the familiar. It's that moment when you no longer feel trapped. It's that moment when you, for once, see what it feels like to fall completely in love with yourself, your life, your work. It's that moment when you feel a strength that you've never felt.

It's the moment when your truth lifts you so high above the world below that you realize you were created to fly.

As you move through these pages, I want you to remember what it feels like to be alive. I don't mean just breathing, I mean *inhaling*. Feeling emotions like excitement, joy, wonder, and passion. You know the stuff that you came into this

#UNCLONED THOUGHTS

PLEASE DOCUMENT YOUR UNCLONED THOUGHTS HERE.
THIS IS YOUR SAFE SPACE

_____

_____

_____

_____

_____

_____

_____

_____

_____

_____

_____

_____

_____

INTRODUCTION

world with. The stuff that life and all of its expectations and pressures and rules robbed you of. The stuff that your spirit is aching for. *That stuff.* Open yourself to reconnecting to that again. Because you deserve it.

More than anything else, I want you to live out your truth. I want you to be true to your commitment—your right—to be who you want to be. I want you to fight for that and protect it with everything you have. I want you to refuse to relinquish your power to be an individual, and to get pissed off at anybody who tries to challenge it. I want you to get so fired up that you refuse to live one more day—one more second—without breathing the oxygen of freedom. I want you to release yourself from the confines of conformity, and sign your own permission slip to be one hundred percent authentic and true to who you are.

#UNCLONED THOUGHTS

PLEASE DOCUMENT YOUR UNCLONED THOUGHTS HERE.
THIS IS YOUR SAFE SPACE

_____

_____

_____

_____

_____

_____

_____

_____

_____

_____

_____

_____

_____

_____

_____

INTRODUCTION

I want you to follow your fucking dreams without looking back or around or beside you for agreement and acceptance. Because there is no other option.

I want you to be Uncommon. I want you to be Unexpected, Unprecedented, Unruly, and Uncompromising.

I want you to be **UnCloned.**

So here's a huge glass of water and your red pill.

Swallow and follow me down this rabbit hole.

#UNCLONED THOUGHTS

PLEASE DOCUMENT YOUR UNCLONED THOUGHTS HERE.
THIS IS YOUR SAFE SPACE

_____

_____

_____

_____

_____

_____

_____

_____

_____

_____

_____

_____

_____

INTRODUCTION

UnCloned

adjective

the space of owning your shit: a state of being in which rules are nonexistent, where restriction is unheard of and you emphatically, undeniably, don't give a fuck

I don't need your permission to be great. But, you need my permission to take my greatness away, and you're not qualified to do that.

-K Elle Jones

(Un)Rule One

#UNCLONED THOUGHTS

PLEASE DOCUMENT YOUR UNCLONED THOUGHTS HERE.
THIS IS YOUR SAFE SPACE

_____

_____

_____

_____

_____

_____

_____

_____

_____

_____

_____

_____

_____

_____

(UN)RULE NUMBER ONE

RECALL EVERYTHING THEY'VE EVER TOLD YOU (AND THEN FORGET IT)

If you've ever sat at a playground on a sunny day and watched children play their little hearts out, you know they are rarely out of the watchful eye of *very* safety-conscious moms. While those mothers appear to be dialed into their animated conversations with the other parents, or reading the books they packed along with the sippy cups, sunscreen, and Neosporin, you immediately know when one of those kids look like they even want to think about doing some remotely dangerous, like…umm…playing. You'll hear that mother shrieking at the top of her lungs, a familiar chorus of sounds that can be heard from the park bench to the Bahamas.

"Johhhhnny! Stop it! You'll fall and hurt yourself!"

"Come back here! You're going too far!"

"No! Don't jump on that!"

#UNCLONED THOUGHTS

PLEASE DOCUMENT YOUR UNCLONED THOUGHTS HERE.
THIS IS YOUR SAFE SPACE

(UN)RULE NUMBER ONE

RECALL EVERYTHING THEY'VE EVER TOLD YOU (AND THEN FORGET IT)

The look on Johnny's face? Priceless. His response? Reckless. He is a daredevil. A risk taker. Hell, a modern-day superhero. You watch as he contemplates taking his life into his own 6-year-old hands. With his chest heaving, you watch as Super Johnny and his mom lock eyes. It's a showdown. Should he stop? Yes. But does he? No. Instead of stopping, Johnny only becomes more daring. He runs faster and climbs higher.

This, ladies and gents, is getting good.

With your "Ooooooh-he's-about-to-get-his-ass-whooped" antennas up and tuned into the much-needed excitement, you casually turn your head, your gaze bouncing back and forth between Mommy and Johnny to watch this movie play out. You should be on Mommy's side, but the advocate in you rises up. Maybe the scene flashes you right back to the

#UNCLONED THOUGHTS

PLEASE DOCUMENT YOUR UNCLONED THOUGHTS HERE.
THIS IS YOUR SAFE SPACE

_____

_____

_____

_____

_____

_____

_____

_____

_____

_____

_____

_____

(UN)RULE NUMBER ONE

RECALL EVERYTHING THEY'VE EVER TOLD YOU (AND THEN FORGET IT)

many times that your own mother snatched the life and breath out of your body for turning your listening ears off in public and you're now living vicariously through this kid, but secretly, you're cheering him on. His defiance feels right and, honestly, justifiable. Johnny's mom has lost sight of the fact that her cub is as safe as can be and, while you aren't a proponent of disrespecting elders, especially parents, you know that little Johnny just wants to be happy and free. You watch in both amusement and awe as Johnny takes off into the wind, with his frantic mother racing behind him.

Atta-boy, Johnny!

Remember this kid. He will probably be your president in the next twenty years. The moral of the story?

Get a heart like Johnny's.

#UNCLONED THOUGHTS

PLEASE DOCUMENT YOUR UNCLONED THOUGHTS HERE.
THIS IS YOUR SAFE SPACE

_____

_____

_____

_____

_____

_____

_____

_____

_____

_____

_____

_____

_____

_____

_____

(UN)RULE NUMBER ONE

RECALL EVERYTHING THEY'VE EVER TOLD YOU (AND THEN FORGET IT)

Let me explain.

From the moment that we come into this world, we are subject to someone else's rules around who and what we should be, and what our norm should look and feel like. Doctors, "experts", and teachers toss information and standards in the air, and our parents, bless their hearts, grab as much of it as they can. Out of the mouths and minds of the world come the benchmarks for how tall we should be, how many teeth we should have, and how soon we should be able to sound out certain words. Being the good, kind people they are, our mothers and fathers take that big ol' ball of stats, and out of fear of having a less-than-spectacular-kid to brag about to their family and coworkers, they run with it. And so it begins—life as we know it. The right schools. The right grades. The right job. The right house, spouse, and car. Completely cloned.

#UNCLONED THOUGHTS

PLEASE DOCUMENT YOUR UNCLONED THOUGHTS HERE.
THIS IS YOUR SAFE SPACE

_____

_____

_____

_____

_____

_____

_____

_____

_____

_____

_____

_____

_____

_____

(UN)RULE NUMBER ONE

RECALL EVERYTHING THEY'VE EVER TOLD YOU (AND THEN FORGET IT)

Our lives are shaped by one set of rules and expectations after the next. From the playground, to the church pew, to your teenaged bedroom, to the dorm room, to your first apartment—you move from place to place, thing to thing, simply because that is the blueprint that has been defined for you. Everything from what you eat, to how you dress, to where you work, to who you hang out with is likely driven by some outside influence or someone's opinion. You've been built by your culture and your environment—where you were born, where you went to school, where you chose to live. Each of those factors became a piece of you. You don't know who you really are.

You're doing what you're doing because somebody told you to or it's the way everyone else has done it before you.

#UNCLONED THOUGHTS

PLEASE DOCUMENT YOUR UNCLONED THOUGHTS HERE.
THIS IS YOUR SAFE SPACE

_____

_____

_____

_____

_____

_____

_____

_____

_____

_____

_____

_____

_____

_____

(UN)RULE NUMBER ONE

RECALL EVERYTHING THEY'VE EVER TOLD YOU (AND THEN FORGET IT)

So that is why your first step to become UnCloned is to deconstruct. Strip. Tear down everything you are so you can become who you need to be.

Forget the rules. Forget what you've learned in school. Forget what you've been told about right or wrong. Forget what Momma, Daddy, The Bestie, and the Hubby said. Forget the likes on social media.

Being liked has no place here.

You don't need to be liked. To be liked is to be tolerated. To be liked is to be accepted by other people, for a fleeting moment until the next new, pretty thing comes along. To be liked is to dumb yourself down, to diminish your shine, to downplay your dopeness so you can make someone else feel brighter.

#UNCLONED THOUGHTS

PLEASE DOCUMENT YOUR UNCLONED THOUGHTS HERE.
THIS IS YOUR SAFE SPACE

(UN)RULE NUMBER ONE

RECALL EVERYTHING THEY'VE EVER TOLD YOU (AND THEN FORGET IT)

No, you don't need to be liked. You need to be loved. Loved by yourself and loved by the people who get you and what you believe to be true.

Evaluate Your Beliefs

What do you believe and why? Are you going to law school because it's considered a respectable profession? Are you only wearing pantyhose because your grandmother always said they're ladylike? Are you living in a certain high-priced neighborhood because it's where six-figure earners are supposed to live? Are you only creating online courses because every other coach is doing it?

If you really deconstruct your core beliefs, one by one, and take a hard, honest look at each, you'll probably find that each of them was shaped by some outside influence. It may be as strong as what your family or church taught you about

#UNCLONED THOUGHTS

PLEASE DOCUMENT YOUR UNCLONED THOUGHTS HERE.
THIS IS YOUR SAFE SPACE

(UN)RULE NUMBER ONE

RECALL EVERYTHING THEY'VE EVER TOLD YOU (AND THEN FORGET IT)

what's right or wrong, or something as subtle as an article that offers "ten ways to do this or that."

Find your core. Figure out what you believe and fully embrace that.

Be radical in this space. Look at everything from your religion to your red lipstick. If it confines or restricts you, let it go. If it only exists in your life because somebody else said so, let it go.

Studying is a Secret Code for Copying

When we like or admire someone, we want to soak up everything we can about them. That person excites us and brings us to life, so we want as much of them as we can access. We follow them on Instagram. We read their auto-

#UNCLONED THOUGHTS

PLEASE DOCUMENT YOUR UNCLONED THOUGHTS HERE.
THIS IS YOUR SAFE SPACE

(UN)RULE NUMBER ONE

RECALL EVERYTHING THEY'VE EVER TOLD YOU (AND THEN FORGET IT)

biographies. We religiously watch every television interview we can find to hear how they speak and the words they use. We want to know how they live and eat. What books they've read. What Facebook groups they belong to. We do everything we can to emulate their behavior, believing that if we do, we can duplicate their success.

Yet in the same breath, we proclaim, "I'm doing me!"

But are you really?

You are here to be the carbon, not the copy. You don't need to become the black, white, Latina, Asian, or African version of anybody else.

Just be you.

#UNCLONED THOUGHTS

PLEASE DOCUMENT YOUR UNCLONED THOUGHTS HERE.
THIS IS YOUR SAFE SPACE

(UN)RULE NUMBER ONE

RECALL EVERYTHING THEY'VE EVER TOLD YOU (AND THEN FORGET IT)

Where You Come From Does Not Determine Who You Are

The world will have you believe that because you don't come from a "normal" family structure or background that you're lost and worthless. If you're not a college-educated Christian, there is no way you can be successful. If you are a single mom, there is no way you can raise healthy, happy children. You're counted out before you can even begin. People have packaged and labeled you as a nobody. You're judged and written off.

Those myths and lies were constructed to strangle the power out of you. If you give in to any of that, if you believe one word of it, they've won.

#UNCLONED THOUGHTS

PLEASE DOCUMENT YOUR UNCLONED THOUGHTS HERE.
THIS IS YOUR SAFE SPACE

_____

_____

_____

_____

_____

_____

_____

_____

_____

_____

_____

_____

_____

(UN)RULE NUMBER ONE

RECALL EVERYTHING THEY'VE EVER TOLD YOU (AND THEN FORGET IT)

We All Win on Our Own Accord

Winning is relative, just like success. You get to define life for you, not on anybody else's terms. A win for you may be owning a fancy car and a condo in a high-rise, while winning for someone else may be couch hopping and backpacking all over the world to do missions work. You can't allow others to shit on your wins. Have the heart (also known as balls) to live how you wanna live.

You don't need to copy when

you are the carbon

- Audria Richmond

(Un)Rule Two

#UNCLONED THOUGHTS

PLEASE DOCUMENT YOUR UNCLONED THOUGHTS HERE.
THIS IS YOUR SAFE SPACE

_____

_____

_____

_____

_____

_____

_____

_____

_____

_____

_____

_____

_____

_____

_____

(UN)RULE NUMBER TWO

EMBRACE CHANGE

Imagine you are getting into your car to head home after a long day. You're exhausted, annoyed, and all you can think about is hopping into some pajamas and bouncing from the front door to the kitchen to the couch. In that order. You turn the car on, set your music, and head out of the parking lot as you always do. Since you know the route so well, you don't think much about the traffic that's building up in front of you. Before you know it, you are smack in front of a dead end and a carnival of orange cones and Detour signs. You yell out one of the few, four-letter words that can properly capture your frustration in the moment. Pissed, you follow your GPS's voice down a windy, unknown road. Reluctantly accepting the fact there is absolutely nothing you can do about the situation, you settle into the flow of the ride and try to relax. Along the way you discover some spots you've never seen before. A library. A community pool. A few

#UNCLONED THOUGHTS

PLEASE DOCUMENT YOUR UNCLONED THOUGHTS HERE.
THIS IS YOUR SAFE SPACE

_____

_____

_____

_____

_____

_____

_____

_____

_____

_____

_____

_____

_____

_____

_____

(UN)RULE NUMBER TWO

EMBRACE CHANGE

trees. *Imagine that.*

Before long, the scenery surrounding you starts to change. Things begin to look more familiar to you. Within a few minutes, you're in your own neighborhood. Finally you're home. Ten minutes earlier than usual.

This route had been here the entire time, but, for years, you've done it the way you've always done it. One way in and one way out. You'd become so accustomed to your way of doing things that it never dawned on you that there may be a better, faster, more enjoyable way home.

Be willing to detour. You never know where that path will lead you. Exploring new spaces, thoughts, and ideas is a good and necessary thing. You get to see through a different, clearer lens. If you feel pulled towards Buddhist principles, flip through a few books or talk to someone

#UNCLONED THOUGHTS

PLEASE DOCUMENT YOUR UNCLONED THOUGHTS HERE.
THIS IS YOUR SAFE SPACE

_____

_____

_____

_____

_____

_____

_____

_____

_____

_____

_____

_____

_____

(UN)RULE NUMBER TWO

EMBRACE CHANGE

who practices the faith. If you've always wanted to try Thai or Ethiopian food, but you've been hesitant for whatever reason, make that tonight's dinner. It may be the worst thing you've ever laid your tongue on, and that's okay. Spit it out and go grab a burger. But what if you discover that this is the most amazing food you've ever had in your life? And because you love it so much, your curiosity leads you to similar restaurants in your city, and then a few states over, and before you know it, you're planning a trip across the globe to fully immerse yourself in the food, culture, and life of other ethnicities. What if?

Free your mind and let your heart and spirit follow.

Go do the craziest, most off-the-wall thing you can think of.

Erase the Notion of Familiarity

#UNCLONED THOUGHTS

PLEASE DOCUMENT YOUR UNCLONED THOUGHTS HERE.
THIS IS YOUR SAFE SPACE

(UN)RULE NUMBER TWO

EMBRACE CHANGE

Resist the urge to run back to the safety and sanctity of the familiar. If you don't shake shit up, you'll never change. Yes, it is a lot of goddamn work to change and to let go of everything, and maybe everybody, that you know. But focus less on what you're leaving behind and more on what's waiting for you. Here, the air tastes different. The people look funny. The food, the clothes, the music, the books—it's all new. And it's right where you belong.

Shit may get a little messy along this path. Your world, as you know it, will be flipped upside down and nothing will feel right or real anymore. Don't worry. It's a really, really good thing.

Failure is not Finite

Once you accept that change is good, you can take the pressure off yourself when it comes to failure. See failure

#UNCLONED THOUGHTS

PLEASE DOCUMENT YOUR UNCLONED THOUGHTS HERE.
THIS IS YOUR SAFE SPACE

(UN)RULE NUMBER TWO

EMBRACE CHANGE

for what it is—some shit you did that just didn't work out. You will screw stuff up, and, guess what? You'll do it again. And again.

You will fail a class. You will get fired from a job. Your business idea will flop. You may get divorced.

Failure is such a beautiful mirror. It reflects what you need to change right away. It reveals where you need more boundaries, what you need to release, and where you need to shift and start something new.

Failure is not the end. In fact, in many instances, failure is your beginning.

The key to handling failure is to accept it at face value. Maybe it was your fault, but likely it wasn't. Redefine your results, but there is no need to redefine yourself. Tweak the

#UNCLONED THOUGHTS

PLEASE DOCUMENT YOUR UNCLONED THOUGHTS HERE.
THIS IS YOUR SAFE SPACE

(UN)RULE NUMBER TWO

EMBRACE CHANGE

shit and try it again. You may just had the most humiliating moment of your life. Go to bed, wake up the next day, and you have another damn shot. Take it.

Embrace the Unknown

Okay. So you're staring this new way of thinking, seeing, and believing in the face. It's one thing to see it. It's a completely different challenge to live it. Acknowledging and accepting your truth is useless if you aren't willing to live it out. Be open to trying and testing new things. Hell, be open to creating your own thing. Find your own way. And when you get there, hang out and live a little. Only you'll know if you've taken a wrong turn. Take the exit if you need to. Just don't jump off the road out of fear of falling over a cliff.

And for God sakes, take your damn seatbelt off.

Conformity changes our beautifully colorful world black and white. Rejoice in your uniqueness with your bold, colorful, out of the box beautiful self!

-Veronique Link

(Un)Rule Three

#UNCLONED THOUGHTS

PLEASE DOCUMENT YOUR UNCLONED THOUGHTS HERE.
THIS IS YOUR SAFE SPACE

(UN)RULE NUMBER THREE

ALWAYS TRUST THE PERSON WHO KNOWS YOU BEST—YOURSELF

When I jumped, feet first, into the deep end of online entrepreneurship in 2014, it was the undoing of all the work that I'd done for years to be true to myself and who I was. I was immediately overwhelmed with everyone else in the space, caught up like a doe in the headlights and completely captivated by what I perceived to be success. I would spend (let's be real, waste) hours on end, browsing website after website, video after video, program after program, until I didn't know where my peers' thoughts ended and mine began. I ate comparison for breakfast, lunch, and dinner. With each click of my mousepad, I felt myself slipping further and further away from my own identity and my own voice.

It was (almost) the beginning of my UnCloned end.

What was really interesting to me was that the most super successful influencers in my industry practically begged people to clone them. Their conversations were so seductive, each of them waving swipe files and strategies for a

#UNCLONED THOUGHTS

PLEASE DOCUMENT YOUR UNCLONED THOUGHTS HERE.
THIS IS YOUR SAFE SPACE

(UN)RULE NUMBER THREE

ALWAYS TRUST THE PERSON WHO KNOWS YOU BEST—YOURSELF

fee to lure you in. It was damn near predatory. But like most people who are new to the online world, or business period, I wanted to win so badly, and I was almost willing to do anything to get it. Almost.

I fell for the trap and did what most of us do and started trying to fit in. I tried to replicate the exact same business models to build my business. I created products and services that were close to what I saw everyone else doing out there.

And I hated it.

It got to a point where I felt so resentful and trapped in a matrix that wasn't me. I wasn't fully showing up as myself or infusing enough of my own creativity, ingenuity, or juice into my process. I wasn't honoring my own genius or what I knew my client really wanted and needed from me. I couldn't do it anymore. I decided that the sacrifice of success wasn't worth it if it meant I couldn't get it on my own terms. I start-

#UNCLONED THOUGHTS

PLEASE DOCUMENT YOUR UNCLONED THOUGHTS HERE.
THIS IS YOUR SAFE SPACE

_____

_____

_____

_____

_____

_____

_____

_____

_____

_____

_____

_____

_____

(UN)RULE NUMBER THREE

ALWAYS TRUST THE PERSON WHO KNOWS YOU BEST—YOURSELF

ed trusting myself. I started believing in my own ideas and being willing to flop, knowing that, if it happened, I would just pick myself up and try again. I started disregarding how crazy or ridiculous it looked to anyone else. Product after product, launch after launch, I was on fire. I felt like myself again.

And everybody noticed.

My Facebook inbox was soon flooded with people who wanted to know my secret. The messages all read something like, "Girl, I don't know what you did, but whatever it was, you've been on fire!" and "Your creativity has been through the roof!" I began attracting clients who, like me, were dying to be different. I stopped getting calls from the penny-pinchers who wanted me to make them an imposter of someone else. Instead, people reached out who had a deep, genuine respect for my aesthetic, my work, and most importantly, for my perspective. I drew people in who were

#UNCLONED THOUGHTS

PLEASE DOCUMENT YOUR UNCLONED THOUGHTS HERE.
THIS IS YOUR SAFE SPACE

(UN)RULE NUMBER THREE

ALWAYS TRUST THE PERSON WHO KNOWS YOU BEST—YOURSELF

inspired to do themselves in their own businesses, and who were fearlessly willing to follow me into this unchartered territory of creativity and discovery that neither of us knew where it would lead.

All of that happened because I was willing to trust myself.

How much more dope would the world be if you listened to everyone else less and yourself more?

The Killer Question

I know you've been there before. You come up with the most amazing idea of your life. It gives you butterflies and makes your toes tingle whenever you think about it. It just feels right. This is too good to keep to yourself, so you pick up the phone, call someone who you respect, and utter the most detrimental four words known to creative man:

"What do *you* think?"

AUDRIA RICHMOND #UNCLONED | UNCLONED.LIFE

#UNCLONED THOUGHTS

PLEASE DOCUMENT YOUR UNCLONED THOUGHTS HERE.
THIS IS YOUR SAFE SPACE

(UN)RULE NUMBER THREE

ALWAYS TRUST THE PERSON WHO KNOWS YOU BEST—YOURSELF

So you hold the phone and watch your incredible idea swoosh down the toilet after the person shits all over it.

Never forget that when you seek someone's opinion, you're getting so much more than their thoughts about you or your idea. You're getting their past experiences, failures, limitations, religious and spiritual beliefs, and in essence, their fears.

Someone's voice of caution and concern could very well be the brakes on your extraordinary ascent into the stratosphere of greatness. Think about that.

There is a Big Difference Between Guidance

and Validation

If you honestly don't know how to do something, ask someone who does. But never believe in them more than you believe in yourself. Don't lose yourself in anyone else's teach-

#UNCLONED THOUGHTS

PLEASE DOCUMENT YOUR UNCLONED THOUGHTS HERE.
THIS IS YOUR SAFE SPACE

_____

_____

_____

_____

_____

_____

_____

_____

_____

_____

_____

_____

_____

(UN)RULE NUMBER THREE

ALWAYS TRUST THE PERSON WHO KNOWS YOU BEST—YOURSELF

ing. Always remain true to who you are. You know what you know. Trust what feels good to you and you can never be wrong.

The Ninety Percent (UN) Rule

If there isn't at least ninety percent of you in an idea, go back and dig deeper. Anything less means that you don't trust the thought or yourself enough—yet.

You Have God in You

If you are guided by anything, let it be God. Trusting yourself is acknowledging that you hear God and you're open to following the compass that The Divine has embedded inside of you.

Get in tune with yourself spiritually and allow God to speak to you—intimately and directly. No filters through others needed. No logic required. None of this has to make sense

#UNCLONED THOUGHTS

PLEASE DOCUMENT YOUR UNCLONED THOUGHTS HERE.
THIS IS YOUR SAFE SPACE

_____

_____

_____

_____

_____

_____

_____

_____

_____

_____

_____

_____

_____

_____

(UN)RULE NUMBER THREE

ALWAYS TRUST THE PERSON WHO KNOWS YOU BEST—YOURSELF

to anyone else. Your Higher Power is calling you to be something. *Be that.*

Don't settle for mediocrity.

It's unbecoming.

-Akilah Pitts

(Un)Rule Four

#UNCLONED THOUGHTS

PLEASE DOCUMENT YOUR UNCLONED THOUGHTS HERE.
THIS IS YOUR SAFE SPACE

_____

_____

_____

_____

_____

_____

_____

_____

_____

_____

_____

_____

_____

_____

(UN)RULE NUMBER FOUR

BECOME YOUR ALTER EGO

Michael Jackson. Beyoncé. Stevie Wonder. Prince.

They are household icons for a reason. They have shaken and shaped culture, influencing us in such a way that we cannot imagine a space without them. Their words, songs, and lives have defined us, inspired us, and moved us. We don't know where we would be without their music.

Do you know why?

Because renegades are sexy as fuck.

Each of these artists have turned our worlds upside down because they refuse to be contained. They've thrown caution and care to the wind, left multi-million dollar record and endorsement deals on the table, were damn near willing to die for what they believed in. Their passion. Their voices. Their art. And we see that, we want it. We want that fire, that freedom, that juice. When you hear a Beyoncé or Prince song on the radio, it's about more than lyrics.

#UNCLONED THOUGHTS

PLEASE DOCUMENT YOUR UNCLONED THOUGHTS HERE.
THIS IS YOUR SAFE SPACE

_____

_____

_____

_____

_____

_____

_____

_____

_____

_____

_____

_____

_____

(UN)RULE NUMBER FOUR

BECOME YOUR ALTER EGO

It's about why you want to dance in the car like a maniac without caring who's watching. It's about why you want to run home to your spouse and screw like your life depended on it. It's about what they make you feel like is possible. Through their eyes, you believe that you can live life without inhibition or fear.

That's not magic. That's living UnCloned.

When people experience you in your zone, it's electric. Their UnCloned spirits make you want to throw your hands in the air and say, "Hell, yeah! Me too!" It's a ripple effect. People want to be in the room with other freedom fighters. There is somebody waiting for you to let loose so they can do it too.

Imagine if you decided to come to work naked because that's how you work best. You're sitting at your desk, creating the most epic thing of your life, oblivious to the world around you. It's like heaven. Somebody would be bold enough to ask you, "What in the hell do you think you're

#UNCLONED THOUGHTS

PLEASE DOCUMENT YOUR UNCLONED THOUGHTS HERE.
THIS IS YOUR SAFE SPACE

_____

_____

_____

_____

_____

_____

_____

_____

_____

_____

_____

_____

_____

_____

(UN)RULE NUMBER FOUR

BECOME YOUR ALTER EGO

doing?" And there will be more people, your secret fans, cheering you on from the sidelines. Slowly, they'll start stripping. Before you know it, you've ignited a goddamn revolution.

But first you have to become the person who you've been hiding all of your life.

Often, when we think of an alter ego, it's that taboo, freaky side of us that no one is supposed to know. She is the person we suppress, yet she represents our most authentic selves. It's our alter ego who dances with reckless abandon and couldn't care less who's watching. It's our alter ego who says what we're *really* thinking. It's our alter ego who doesn't play it safe.

And it's our alter ego who is dying to be set free.

A few years ago, Beyoncé introduced a new, sultry side of herself to the world, and she called her "Sasha Fierce."

#UNCLONED THOUGHTS

PLEASE DOCUMENT YOUR UNCLONED THOUGHTS HERE.
THIS IS YOUR SAFE SPACE

_____
_____
_____
_____
_____
_____
_____
_____
_____
_____
_____
_____
_____
_____
_____
_____
_____

(UN)RULE NUMBER FOUR

BECOME YOUR ALTER EGO

While she was always very feminine with her performances, she played it safe, and her off-stage presence depicted a reserved, youthful girl who portrayed the bubble-gum image that was acceptable, non-threating, and comfortable as part of a group, but not necessarily leading one.

Sasha was something else.

She was powerful. She was a dangerously sexy, femme fatale. She was outspoken, daring, and didn't give a shit about what anybody thought. She was a boss. She was a grown woman.

Soon, something happened. As Bey became more comfortable with the woman she always wanted to be, her two identities morphed and she discovered there was no need to hide behind Sasha anymore. She embraced her true self. She and Sasha became one. She became an icon. She became UnCloned.

#UNCLONED THOUGHTS

PLEASE DOCUMENT YOUR UNCLONED THOUGHTS HERE.
THIS IS YOUR SAFE SPACE

(UN)RULE NUMBER FOUR

BECOME YOUR ALTER EGO

Your alter ego is not the person you should hide—it's the person you should be. Stop censoring yourself. Set yourself free.

If you're known for being quiet, unleash your opinions on the world. If you want to curse in public, do that. If you've never been one to dance in public, get in the middle of the floor at the next party.

Become unboxed and unhinged.

If my shine blinds you, please invest in some good sunglasses.

— **Apryl Beverly**

(Un)Rule Five

#UNCLONED THOUGHTS

PLEASE DOCUMENT YOUR UNCLONED THOUGHTS HERE.
THIS IS YOUR SAFE SPACE

_____

_____

_____

_____

_____

_____

_____

_____

_____

_____

_____

_____

_____

_____

(UN)RULE NUMBER FIVE

TO HELL WITH THE INVITES FROM THE COOL KIDS—YOU WEREN'T GOING ANYWAY

As this new version of you begins to emerge, you will feel stronger than you've ever felt in your life. You'll feel ferocious. In control. Ready to take on the world. You'll love the skin you're in.

And everyone else will hate it.

Welcome to The Edge.

Old friends will stop calling. Your mailbox and inbox will be dehydrated when the flow of social invitations dries up. You'll be called selfish, obnoxious, foolish, and insane. You'll receive all kinds of unsolicited feedback and advice from people who'll be scratching their heads and wondering if you've completely gone off the deep end. You have, so they're absolutely right. They're just not tall enough to ride this ride.

The Edge is the decision point. Think of it as the fork in the road, the divider in the pool that separates that oh-I-got-

AUDRIA RICHMOND   #UNCLONED | UNCLONED.LIFE

#UNCLONED THOUGHTS

PLEASE DOCUMENT YOUR UNCLONED THOUGHTS HERE.
THIS IS YOUR SAFE SPACE

(UN)RULE NUMBER FIVE

TO HELL WITH THE INVITES FROM THE COOL KIDS—YOU WEREN'T GOING ANYWAY

this-side from the oh-shit-I-really-can't-swim side, the blue versus the red pill, the moment when you decide if you are going to hit the gas or slam on the brakes, throw the car in reverse, and go back to that boring, dismal, funky life you came from.

This is where you know if you are going to be a sheep or a lion (or a lioness).

The choice is yours.

Let's say you decide to go from your super-safe black hair to a shocking, I-ain't-playing-with-these-bitches blue. As soon as your stylist swirls you around in the chair and you see if for the first time, you can't believe it's taken you this long to do this. You instantly feel lighter, happier, and freer. Yet when you upload your new profile picture, no one bothers to like it. Your cousin texts you, losing it, because it's two weeks before her wedding and there's no way you can be in her pictures looking like *that*. Next, there's a call from your

#UNCLONED THOUGHTS

PLEASE DOCUMENT YOUR UNCLONED THOUGHTS HERE.
THIS IS YOUR SAFE SPACE

_____

_____

_____

_____

_____

_____

_____

_____

_____

_____

_____

_____

_____

_____

_____

(UN)RULE NUMBER FIVE

TO HELL WITH THE INVITES FROM THE COOL KIDS—YOU WEREN'T GOING ANYWAY

mom, wondering how you could be so inconsiderate and embarrass her in front of the entire family. And here you were thinking that it was just hair.

Whether it's your family losing it over a little bleach on your tresses or losing a few hundred Facebook friends after posted a supportive statement for transgender women, the reality is not everyone you know and love will agree with what you say and how you live.

And you can handle that.

Until now, you've been terrified to speak your mind. There are careers you want to explore, causes you want to support, clothes you want to wear, and people who you want to take those clothes off (yes, let's lay it all out there) but you haven't done any of those things out of fear of pissing some people off and losing some people from your life. Your biggest fear is not blue hair or bad sex. It's not losing your job or a leg.

AUDRIA RICHMOND   #UNCLONED | UNCLONED.LIFE

#UNCLONED THOUGHTS

PLEASE DOCUMENT YOUR UNCLONED THOUGHTS HERE.
THIS IS YOUR SAFE SPACE

(UN)RULE NUMBER FIVE

TO HELL WITH THE INVITES FROM THE COOL KIDS—YOU WEREN'T GOING ANYWAY

It's being alone.

This is another shift in your perspective. You may feel lonely, but a silent space is not the worst thing that could possibly happen to you. Silence is weird—until you get used to it. Stop running from quiet and get into it. Turn off the stuff that penetrates your brain and *think*. Plan. Draw or color. Run around naked with the shades up. Have church service in your living room in your underwear. Wear stilettos and sweatpants. Go the movies or dinner by yourself. Buy a single, roundtrip ticket and travel somewhere you've never been. You just may come back as someone new.

The Most Important Kind of Love

Some of us feel incomplete without friends. Some of us feel lost without family or children. Others feel a desperate need for a spouse or romantic partner. And that desire often drives us to stay in situations and scenarios that can kill us—emotionally and spiritually. They create these deep

#UNCLONED THOUGHTS

PLEASE DOCUMENT YOUR UNCLONED THOUGHTS HERE.
THIS IS YOUR SAFE SPACE

_____

_____

_____

_____

_____

_____

_____

_____

_____

_____

_____

_____

_____

_____

(UN)RULE NUMBER FIVE

TO HELL WITH THE INVITES FROM THE COOL KIDS—YOU WEREN'T GOING ANYWAY

holes that only attention and validation from another person can fill. We are constantly not at peace. Unsupported. Unloved. Stomped on. Yes that's what happens when we allow assholes into our intimate spaces. But they can only slither in when there's a hole to fill. They get in when we're empty.

A sense of wholeness can only come from the love that you give yourself. When you are so solid on the love you give yourself, when you place yourself on a pedestal, then you can be full.

Who Would You Love?

If religion, race, education, financial status, or looks weren't a concern, who would you love? If you woke up tomorrow and the world was just one big, open space, who would you strike up a conversation with in line at the grocery store? Who would you kiss if no one was watching? Who would you play basketball with, discuss your favorite television show or book with, or invite to Thanksgiving dinner if you had no fear

#UNCLONED THOUGHTS

PLEASE DOCUMENT YOUR UNCLONED THOUGHTS HERE.
THIS IS YOUR SAFE SPACE

(UN)RULE NUMBER FIVE

TO HELL WITH THE INVITES FROM THE COOL KIDS—YOU WEREN'T GOING ANYWAY

of judgement?

Find those people. Love them and allow them to love you in return.

When I lived in Memphis, there was a tribe of die-hard *Lord of the Rings* fanatics. They would all get together in their costumes and meet at these secret locations in the woods for sword fights and hunting and comradery. Some were black and some were white. Some were tall and others were short. There were old, young, women, men, and even some families who participated. It didn't matter what they looked or smelled like—they had a bond between them based on a mutual love for a single thing. That's what love is supposed to be. Freedom. Non-judgement. Crazy and illogical, except to the people involved.

You can find people who love and accept you just as you are. You—you beautiful, quirky, funny, brilliant one who laughs too loud, eats too much, doesn't work out enough,

#UNCLONED THOUGHTS

PLEASE DOCUMENT YOUR UNCLONED THOUGHTS HERE.
THIS IS YOUR SAFE SPACE

_____

_____

_____

_____

_____

_____

_____

_____

_____

_____

_____

_____

_____

_____

_____

(UN)RULE NUMBER FIVE

TO HELL WITH THE INVITES FROM THE COOL KIDS—YOU WEREN'T GOING ANYWAY

and changes careers like you change your underwear. Yes, you. All of you. Every piece of you. Every ounce of you.

If you stop holding a place and space for the people who judge you, the people who tell you that you aren't enough, the people who you have to turn yourself inside out and upside down to please, the people who don't understand why your brain moves the way it does, the people who discourage you from loving yourself, you can make room for the ones who should be there.

Venture into the woods and find your people.

The Truth About Shining

Be honest. You've always had this feeling that you were different, better than *them*. It has nothing to do with clothes or cash or college, either. It's the feeling, deep down in your soul, that you saw things bigger. Brighter. You wanted to be more. You wanted to touch, feel, and smell different things.

#UNCLONED THOUGHTS

PLEASE DOCUMENT YOUR UNCLONED THOUGHTS HERE.
THIS IS YOUR SAFE SPACE

_____

_____

_____

_____

_____

_____

_____

_____

_____

_____

_____

_____

_____

_____

_____

(UN)RULE NUMBER FIVE

TO HELL WITH THE INVITES FROM THE COOL KIDS—YOU WEREN'T GOING ANYWAY

And you've been seeking circles all of your life where people felt like that too. You'd get in, start hanging out a bit, and as soon as you thought to yourself, *Hey, I like it here. They finally get it*, the room goes quiet.

You're too loud. You think you know everything. You think you're better and smarter than the rest of us. You're always talking about some crazy idea. Why can't you just get a job? Have some kids? Stop screwing around? Stop chanting. Stop praying. Stop studying. Stop creating. Just stop.

This is what shining feels like. It feels like being in room filled with people who can't even find the right pair of sunglasses to look at you because you're so bright. You can't help it. You. Just. Are.

DAMNIT, can you stop shining?

Nah, fuck that. Burn their asses. And toss them some sunscreen on your way up.

Never take a "no" from someone

who can't give you a "yes"

-Jasmine Turner

(Un)Rule Six

#UNCLONED THOUGHTS

PLEASE DOCUMENT YOUR UNCLONED THOUGHTS HERE.
THIS IS YOUR SAFE SPACE

_____

_____

_____

_____

_____

_____

_____

_____

_____

_____

_____

_____

_____

_____

_____

(UN)RULE NUMBER SIX

QUESTION THE QUESTIONS

Your life should be a constant state of evolution, learning, and seeking. Be infinitely and unapologetically curious. Follow your inner compass.

That is a very lovely, philosophical way of saying this:

Keep your eye on the bullshit ball.

Refuse to take everything for face value. You have people who live their entire lives by what they see on the news, by what they read in their interpreted Bibles or hear their rabbi say, or what the latest business guru spews as truth. Society teaches us that this is the way to live—find a leader, find a source, find someone who you think is smarter than you—and let them lead you around by the balls and tell you how to live your life. *Uh uh.* You are better than some brainless zombie. Do your own damn math. Put your own pieces of the puzzle together.

And if your definition of truth and facts aligns with what

#UNCLONED THOUGHTS

PLEASE DOCUMENT YOUR UNCLONED THOUGHTS HERE.
THIS IS YOUR SAFE SPACE

_____

_____

_____

_____

_____

_____

_____

_____

_____

_____

_____

_____

_____

_____

(UN)RULE NUMBER SIX

QUESTION THE QUESTIONS

other people are saying in the world (sometimes that happens) then roll with it. If it doesn't, then don't. You have a right to call bullshit when you see it.

There will always be somebody who wants to challenge your beliefs. They'll relentlessly press you for facts, stats, and back-up to validate your opinions and ideas. They'll pull out their dictionaries, religious texts, and newspapers in an attempt to bully you into submission. They'll use your weaknesses, your insecurities, your fears against you. The answer to that?

Don't have any.

A difference in perspective doesn't make you less than. Going against the grain and refusing to allow someone to overshadow your feelings and thoughts doesn't make you stupid. In fact, it makes you fucking brilliant.

It's not a coincidence that when extraordinary minds need

#UNCLONED THOUGHTS

PLEASE DOCUMENT YOUR UNCLONED THOUGHTS HERE.
THIS IS YOUR SAFE SPACE

_____

_____

_____

_____

_____

_____

_____

_____

_____

_____

_____

_____

(Un)Rule Seven

#UNCLONED THOUGHTS

PLEASE DOCUMENT YOUR UNCLONED THOUGHTS HERE.
THIS IS YOUR SAFE SPACE

_____

_____

_____

_____

_____

_____

_____

_____

_____

_____

_____

_____

_____

_____

(UN)RULE NUMBER SEVEN

UNNICHE YOUR LIFE

One of the biggest misconceptions about life is that we have to be and do one thing. We have to choose one career, one life partner, one city to live in, one car to drive. Society teaches us that we can't have two things at once. It's blasphemy to say that you want it all.

No it's not blasphemy. It's bullshit.

The truth is you can do whatever you want to do and be whoever you want to be. I know that sounds cliché, but it's the truth that you've always heard, yet never felt that was really possible for you. Out of fear of letting someone down, being seen as a weirdo or heaven forbid, *different*, you boxed yourself into this safe, single-lane life, watching the world from the sidelines.

You have always wanted to write a movie script, but you have a degree in education, so teaching it is. You have this passion for travel, but everyone in your family is deathly afraid of airplanes, so you never fly. You can write, draw,

#UNCLONED THOUGHTS

PLEASE DOCUMENT YOUR UNCLONED THOUGHTS HERE.
THIS IS YOUR SAFE SPACE

_____

_____

_____

_____

_____

_____

_____

_____

_____

_____

_____

_____

_____

_____

_____

_____

_____

(UN)RULE NUMBER SEVEN

UNNICHE YOUR LIFE

code, and create a business plan, but you're only supposed to choose one business idea...

Bullshit.

Look at Jamie Foxx. He sings. He plays piano. He is a dynamic actor and can play roles from beloved musical legends to hated comic book villains. Rarely do you hear anyone say that he should pick one thing and do that. No, in fact it's just the opposite. We praise him for his talent. He refuses to be limited and restricted, and the world bows to his will.

Artists like Pharrell Williams, Issa Rae, and Jidenna refuse to be niched. They shake the culture and cross boundaries that many of us are afraid to. It's beyond the music or art they create. It's their minds and ideas. It's their style and how they wear their hair. It's their willingness to experiment while the whole world watches.

AUDRIA RICHMOND   #UNCLONED | UNCLONED.LIFE

#UNCLONED THOUGHTS

PLEASE DOCUMENT YOUR UNCLONED THOUGHTS HERE.
THIS IS YOUR SAFE SPACE

_____

_____

_____

_____

_____

_____

_____

_____

_____

_____

_____

_____

_____

_____

_____

_____

(UN)RULE NUMBER SEVEN

UNNICHE YOUR LIFE

On the spiritual tip, God gave you every talent and every gift that dwells inside of you. If it wasn't meant for you to have—and use—why is it there? Why would you be so damn good at something, but no one was ever supposed to see, know, or experience it?

What if you were born to be a piano-playing-cake-baking-teacher? What if you were born to build a church, but you love hip-hop and tattoos? What if the most amazing life is not inside of a classroom or a cubicle or with children of your own?

What if you just want to live?

You don't have to pick one crayon to color or one toy to play with anymore. Take the whole fucking box. Be the cowboy and the princess. And if you change your mind tomorrow, change it. You have the right to explore. You have the right to be multi-talented. You have the right to redefine yourself. You have the right to scrap everything you have and every-

#UNCLONED THOUGHTS

PLEASE DOCUMENT YOUR UNCLONED THOUGHTS HERE.
THIS IS YOUR SAFE SPACE

_____

_____

_____

_____

_____

_____

_____

_____

_____

_____

_____

_____

_____

_____

(UN)RULE NUMBER SEVEN

UNNICHE YOUR LIFE

thing you know, get rid of what doesn't feel right anymore, and start all over again. You have the right to have it all.

Now, go do it.

Join the Movement

Are you ready to UnClone Your Life?

If so, you are in the right place because you have just completed this book. This book is the starting point of a conversation that has to happen in our society. I really want you to take this book and use it as your manifesto and journal. I want you to make reference to it all the time, keep coming back to read it again and again when you don't want to confine to society needs, and when you feel like you can't be yourself or trust your ideas.

Now, the next thing I need you to do is join the movement so you can stay plugged in to updates, activities, and special events.

It's so many ways that you can join the movement. Please review the links on the next couple of pages.

UnCloned Life

Website

www.uncloned.life

Podcast

www.unclonedpodcast.com

UnCloned Life Tribe

www.unclonedtribe.life

Facebook

https://www.facebook.com/unclonedlife/

Instagram

https://www.instagram.com/UnClonedLife/

Twitter

https://twitter.com/unclonedlife

Periscope

https://www.periscope.tv/unclonedlife

Email

info@uncloned.life

Founder of UnCloned Life Audria Richmond

Website

www.audriarichmond.com

Facebook

https://www.facebook.com/audriadrichmond/

Instagram

https://www.instagram.com/audriarichmond/

Twitter

https://twitter.com/audriarichmond

Periscope

https://www.periscope.tv/audriarichmond/

YouTube

https://www.youtube.com/user/audriarichmond

Until next time, let's Go UnClone Your Life!

Love,

Audria Richmond

ABOUT THE AUTHOR

She is a self-titled, results-validated Branding and Marketing Genius. She is a pace setter, a needle mover, and an industry fire starter. She is a woman with a master plan, a marketer with a message, and the brains behind the brands of several industry influencers in the online realm.

She is Audria Richmond.

Audria is the founder of the Building Big Brands Agency, an award-winning branding and marketing consultancy for top-notch brands who want to command first-rate profits. As a highly sought after consultant, Audria champions entrepreneurs to stand in front of their brands—uncloned and unafraid to be seen. With her incomparable formula of innovation, unquenchable creativity, and tech-savviness, Audria is a force that is impossible to reckon with. In 2016, she helped her clients to reel in over $1 million in profits and she's left her mark on personal and company brands all over the world, from the United States to Singapore.

Audria changed the game with her signature system, *UnCloned: The Seven Phases of a Profitable Personal Brand*, a revolutionary system that teaches clients how to build wildly profitable personal brands from the ground up with the proven practices, the tools, and the strategies they need to go big and stay there. Recently, she added best-selling author to her portfolio of accolades with the release of her debut book, *Are You Ready for the Yes: How to Prep Your Brand for Lucrative Opportunities*.

ARE YOU READY FOR THE Yes?

HOW TO PREP YOUR PERSONAL BRAND FOR *Lucrative Opportunities*

AUDRIA RICHMOND
BRANDING & MARKETING GENIUS

Your Name is Worth Millions

If you've ever wondered why the expert-next-door is getting the cash and the clients while you secretly hate from the sidelines, this is the book for you.

Imagine that moment when the phone rings with the opportunity of a lifetime. Whether it's your first big client, that incredible book deal with a major publisher, or a speaking engagement at a conference in your city, your ducks need to be in a row long before the dollars show up on your doorstep. You want the visibility and the profits that come with it but are you **really** playing at a level that sets you up for the spotlight?

In this much-anticipated book, Personal Branding and Marketing Genius Audria Richmond cracks the code to building a brand one doable and deliberate step at a time. From creating an authentic personal brand to landing the right media opportunities, Audria's transparent, in-your-face-and-in-your-bank-account approach will help you to:

Develop **ferocious confidence** and show up on the business scene like a boss.

Identify **the people who need your services and demand** the premium rates you deserve.

Understand the **7 Phases of a Profitable Personal Brand** and how to leverage each of them to become the must-meet expert in your industry.

By the end of *ARE YOU READY FOR THE YES?*, you ll finally get out there and make some noise and make some real money at the same damn time.

Order Your Copy Today at www.areyoureadyfortheyesbook.com

UNCLONED LIFE

SHOP ONLINE NOW AT
WWW.UNCLONEDLIFE.SHOP

www.ingramcontent.com/pod-product-compliance
Lightning Source LLC
Chambersburg PA
CBHW060135100426
42744CB00007B/794